National Parks
Grand Canyon

JOSH GREGORY

Children's Press®
An Imprint of Scholastic Inc.

Content Consultant
James Gramann, PhD
Professor, Department of Recreation, Park and Tourism Sciences
Texas A&M University, College Station, Texas

Library of Congress Cataloging-in-Publication Data

Names: Gregory, Josh, author.
Title: Grand Canyon / by Josh Gregory.
Description: New York, NY : Children's Press, an imprint of Scholastic Inc.,
  [2017] | Series: A true book | Includes bibliographical references and index.
Identifiers: LCCN 2016049426 | ISBN 9780531233931 (library binding) | ISBN
  9780531240205 (pbk.)
Subjects: LCSH: Grand Canyon National Park (Ariz.)—Juvenile literature.
Classification: LCC F788 .G776 2017 | DDC 979.1/32—dc23
LC record available at https://lccn.loc.gov/2016049426

All rights reserved. Published in 2018 by Children's Press, an imprint of Scholastic Inc.
Printed in China 62

SCHOLASTIC, CHILDREN'S PRESS, A TRUE BOOK™, and associated logos are trademarks and/or
registered trademarks of Scholastic Inc., 557 Broadway, New York, NY 10012.
1 2 3 4 5 6 7 8 9 10 R 27 26 25 24 23 22 21 20 19 18

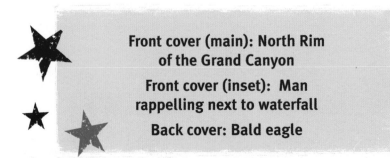

**Front cover (main): North Rim
of the Grand Canyon**

**Front cover (inset): Man
rappelling next to waterfall**

Back cover: Bald eagle

Find the Truth!

Everything you are about to read is true *except* for one of the sentences on this page.

Which one is **TRUE**?

T or F Temperatures at the bottom of the canyon are colder than those higher up.

T or F The Grand Canyon is 1 mile (1.6 kilometers) deep on average.

Find the answers in this book.

Contents

THE **BIG** TRUTH!

National Park Field Guide: Grand Canyon

Bald eagle

4

The Colorado River in the Grand Canyon

A hiker

Be careful! Falling is a serious danger at the Grand Canyon. Never get too close to the edge.

CHAPTER 1

A Grand History

As you peer out over the railing, you almost can't believe your eyes. You've seen pictures of the Grand Canyon before, but seeing it for real is so much more amazing! The canyon's walls are lined with colorful stripes of rock. Between the towering walls, far below you, the shining waters of the Colorado River rush along the bottom of the canyon. It is a truly stunning sight!

The Grand Canyon was the 17th national park created in the United States.

Grand Canyon National Park

Many people visit Mather Point, a great spot for views of the park.

Attracting an Audience

Located in northwestern Arizona, the Grand Canyon is one of the most famous natural landforms on Earth. It is known for its incredible views, rich history, and the amazing activities visitors can enjoy there. All this draws huge crowds to Grand Canyon National Park , the 1,904-square mile (4,931-square kilometer) area surrounding the canyon. More than 4.5 million people on average travel there every year from all around the world.

Billions of Years in the Making

To learn about the canyon's history, you can study the layers of rock that make up its massive, sloped walls. Over very long periods of time, each layer formed on top of the previous one. The layers are made up of different kinds of rocks. This is what gives the canyon its unique striped appearance.

The materials that formed the oldest visible rock layer first settled over 2.5 billion years ago!

Youngest rock layers

Oldest rock layers

About six million years ago, the Colorado River began flowing along its present path from the Rocky Mountains in Colorado to the Gulf of California. The water's movement eventually wore a path in the ground. The Grand Canyon slowly formed over millions of years as the river dug this path deeper and deeper over time. Rain, wind, and other forces also caused the canyon's sides to **erode**. This widened it and made its sides slope downward.

A Timeline of Grand Canyon Milestones

6 million years ago

The Colorado River first flows along its current course through what became the Grand Canyon.

12,000 years ago

Humans first move into the Grand Canyon region.

600 CE

The Pai, ancestors of the Hualapai and other native groups, first settle along the Colorado River.

The People of the Canyon

Humans first came to the Grand Canyon about 12,000 years ago. **Archaeologists** have uncovered ancient hunting tools, pottery, and other artifacts in the canyon. Several Native American groups eventually settled in the region. They included the Navajo, the Hualapai, and the Havasupai. Many **descendants** of these groups live near the park today.

1903
President Theodore Roosevelt visits the Grand Canyon. He declares it "the one great sight which every American should see."

1869
Explorer John Wesley Powell leads the first U.S. expedition down the river and through the canyon.

1919
Congress passes a law creating Grand Canyon National Park.

The Grand Canyon became a part of the United States in 1848. It was part of a large portion of land the U.S. government obtained from Mexico as a result of the Mexican-American War (1846–1848). At the time, the land was largely unmapped. Few people outside of the Native Americans who lived there had ever seen the Grand Canyon. European-American explorers began traveling to the new region to study the canyon and the surrounding area.

By the late 1800s, the Grand Canyon had already become a popular tourist attraction. Many people wanted the government to protect the canyon. They knew that too much human activity could ruin its natural beauty. In 1919, Congress voted to make the area a national park. Anyone would be free to visit, but no one would be allowed to own the park's land or build on it.

National Park Fact File

A national park is land that is protected by the federal government. It is a place of importance to the United States because of its beauty, history, or value to scientists. The U.S. Congress creates a national park by passing a law. Here are some key facts about Grand Canyon National Park.

Grand Canyon National Park	
Location	Northwestern Arizona
Year established	1919
Size	1,904 square miles (4,931 square kilometers)
Average number of visitors each year	More than 4.5 million
Widest point of the canyon	18 miles (29 km)
Deepest point of the canyon	6,000 feet (1,829 m)

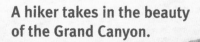

A hiker takes in the beauty of the Grand Canyon.

Well-marked trails allow hikers to easily explore the wonders of the Grand Canyon.

CHAPTER 2

Exploring the Canyon

The first thing you might notice when you reach the canyon is its remarkable size. It stretches on for 277 miles (446 km) of the Colorado River's length. At its widest point, the canyon spans 18 miles (29 km) between its two rims: the North Rim and the South Rim. From the edges of the rims to the river below, the canyon has an average depth of about 1 mile (1.6 km).

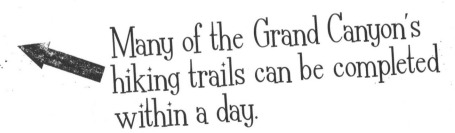

Many of the Grand Canyon's hiking trails can be completed within a day.

The Colorado river flows between the canyon's two rims.

Getting Around

The South Rim is easy to reach by car and is open year-round. This makes it more popular among visitors. The North Rim is much higher and more difficult to reach, and it closes for several months each winter. Its hiking trails are also more challenging.

Helicopter tours offer an exciting way to peer into the canyon from above the rims. These flights last anywhere from 20 minutes to several hours.

A Walk in the Sky

The Skywalk is a glass sidewalk that juts out over the Grand Canyon, 4,000 feet (1,219 m) from the bottom. It is located outside the park in nearby lands that belong to the Hualapai. These native people have lived in the region for centuries. In the 1800s, white settlers took over much of their land. The U.S. government gave some land back in 1883. The Skywalk helps attract tourists, which creates jobs and exposes visitors to Hualapai culture and history.

Members of the Hualapai Nation before the Skywalk opening ceremony in 2012.

Into the Canyon

To enter the canyon itself, many people take a mule ride. Travelers start at one of the canyon's rims. Expert guides lead them to the bottom of the canyon. The entire trip takes about three hours. The journey isn't backbreaking, but it can be rough. The mules travel along pathways carved carefully into the canyon's sloping sides. Along the way, riders see many parts of the canyon that aren't visible from above.

Mules have been carrying visitors into the Grand Canyon since the 1880s.

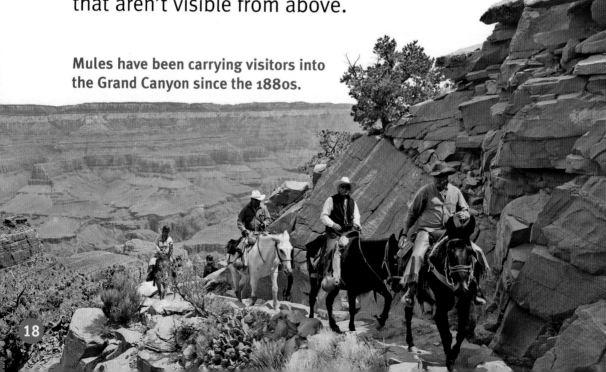

Hot and Cold

At the Grand Canyon, you need to be prepared for different weather conditions. Up on the rims, summer days are mild and nights are cool. But deeper in the canyon, the temperature is warmer. At the bottom, it can heat up to 120 degrees Fahrenheit (49 degrees Celsius) during the summer. In winter, expect very cold temperatures and snow on the rims. However, the warmth inside the canyon melts snow into rain before it reaches the bottom.

Even the tallest buildings in the world would fit easily inside the Grand Canyon.

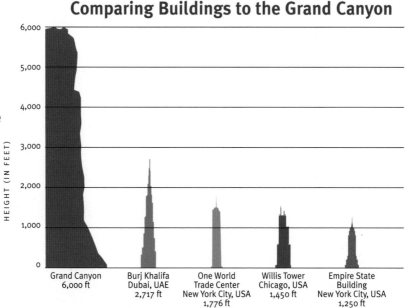

Comparing Buildings to the Grand Canyon

HEIGHT (IN FEET)

6,000
5,000
4,000
3,000
2,000
1,000
0

Grand Canyon
6,000 ft

Burj Khalifa
Dubai, UAE
2,717 ft

One World
Trade Center
New York City, USA
1,776 ft

Willis Tower
Chicago, USA
1,450 ft

Empire State
Building
New York City, USA
1,250 ft

STRUCTURES

Bring your binoculars to enjoy incredible bird-watching at the Grand Canyon.

CHAPTER 3

Creatures Great and Small

As you explore the Grand Canyon, you'll be amazed at the variety of animals you see. Thousands of **species** populate the canyon, from enormous birds to tiny insects. Spotting these animals is one of the coolest parts of visiting the park. However, you should always remember to leave the animals alone. Don't try to feed them, touch them, or even get too close!

Grand Canyon National Park is home to nearly 450 bird species.

California condors can glide for hours looking for carrion, or dead animals, to eat.

Up in the Air

Birds of all kinds are a common sight in Grand Canyon National Park. They range from tiny, insect-eating wrens to huge birds of prey such as bald eagles. The park is even home to the California condor. This is one of the most **endangered** bird species in the world. Its enormous wingspan measures about 9.5 feet (3 meters) across.

Magnificent Mammals

More than 90 **mammal** species roam throughout the park. Small animals such as squirrels and ringtails scurry across tree branches. Bats soar through the night sky. Larger animals such as mule deer, elk, and bison are also easy to find. Mountain lions stalk the park's deer and elk, as well as its smaller mammals. When driving on the park's roads, visitors should keep an eye out for these big cats. They are sometimes hit by cars.

Mountain lions are also known as catamounts, cougars, panthers, pumas, and other names.

Creepy Crawlers

More than 1,440 insect and other **invertebrate** species also live in the park. You might spot butterflies flapping their colorful wings or bees dashing among wildflowers. Huge black beetles crawl across the ground. There are even tarantulas! Enormous and hairy, you'll most likely see these oversize spiders in fall when they leave their burrows to find mates. And while a tarantula bite is not dangerous, make sure to avoid another arachnid, the bark scorpion.

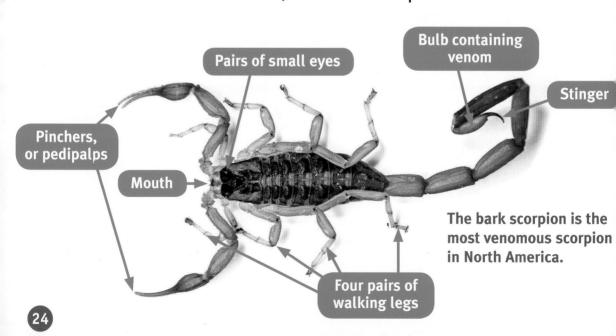

Pairs of small eyes

Bulb containing venom

Stinger

Pinchers, or pedipalps

Mouth

The bark scorpion is the most venomous scorpion in North America.

Four pairs of walking legs

A fisher grabs a rainbow trout from the river.

Creepers, Leapers, and More

Many other kinds of animals can also be found in the park. Reptiles are very common. These include colorful lizards, slow-moving tortoises, and deadly rattlesnakes. Near the Colorado River or other water sources, you will likely spy frogs, toads, and other amphibians. If you wade in a little deeper, you might also find some of the park's five **native** fish species.

THE BIG TRUTH!

National Park Field Guide:
Grand Canyon

Here are a few of the hundreds of fascinating animals you may see in the park.

Canyon tree frog

Scientific name: *Hyla arenicolor*

Habitat: Near streams in forested areas, usually perched on rocks and boulders

Diet: Ants, spiders, beetles, flies, and other small invertebrates

Fact: The inside of their back legs is bright yellow, which can only be seen when the frogs jump.

Mojave rattlesnake

Scientific name: *Crotalus scutulatus*

Habitat: Open rocky areas in the canyon, but sometimes on the rims

Diet: Small animals, including mammals, birds, and reptiles

Fact: The snake's rattle is mostly used to scare away possible attackers.

Gila monster

Scientific name: *Heloderma suspectum*

Habitat: Desert areas in westernmost parts of the park

Diet: Rodents, lizards, bird eggs, and invertebrates

Fact: A gila monster's bite is venomous and painful.

Mule deer

Scientific name: *Odocoileus hemionus*

Habitat: The entire park

Diet: A range of plants, such as grass and shrubs, nuts, and berries

Fact: The mule deer's range extends from Mexico all the way to Alaska.

Desert bighorn sheep

Scientific name: *Ovis canadensis nelsoni*

Habitat: Steep areas and cliffsides

Diet: Grasses and shrubs

Fact: These sheep can perch comfortably on a ledge as little as 2 inches (5 centimeters) wide.

Bald eagle

Scientific name: *Halliaeetus leucocephalus*

Habitat: Usually near water sources

Diet: Fish and smaller birds

Fact: Bald eagles aren't really bald. They're named for the white feathers that cover their heads.

From Forest to Desert

Grand Canyon National Park is most famous for its dramatic rock formations. But it is also home to an incredible variety of plants. Weather conditions and the availability of water vary significantly throughout the park. As a result, there are dramatic changes in the types of plants you see as you explore different areas. You'll find heavily wooded forests, grassy meadows, sparse deserts, and more.

More than 2,000 plant species can be found in Grand Canyon National Park.

Pinyon pines and juniper trees grow along the edges of the North Rim.

Aspen leaves in fall

Tremendous Trees

Forests probably aren't what you picture when you think of the Grand Canyon. However, they are exactly what you'll find up high on many parts of the North and South Rims. Most of the trees are evergreens, such as spruce, fir, and pine. But one deciduous, or non-evergreen tree, stands out. Each fall when the leaves change, bright yellow leaves of the quaking aspen attract visitors to the North Rim.

Hidden Meadows

If you explore the North Rim, you might be lucky enough to see one of the park's few meadows. These beautiful areas are covered in a thick blanket of tall green grasses. They are found high up in the same areas where forests grow and water is plentiful. Different grasses grow in these areas depending on how much water is available.

About a dozen plant species in Grand Canyon National Park cannot be found anywhere else.

Fruit

Spine

Pad

Three basic parts of a prickly pear cactus

Down in the Desert

As you travel farther down into the canyon, the landscape starts to look more like a desert. The weather is hotter here, and there is less water. The landscape is dotted sparsely with a variety of bushes. You'll also see plenty of cacti. These spiky plants thrive in hot, dry environments. When it rains, they soak up as much water as possible and store it for later use.

A redbud tree blooms along the Colorado River inside the canyon.

Along the Riverbanks

If you make it all the way down to the banks of the Colorado River, you'll see a whole new group of plants. Many types of trees, shrubs, and wildflowers can be found here. You might also see leafy ferns. These ancient plants likely first appeared in the Grand Canyon as long as 400 million years ago. This is before any of the other types of plants found there today had begun to grow on Earth.

A Grand Canyon National Park ranger inspects the park.

Protecting the Park

National parks are protected by a variety of laws. These regulations are designed to preserve the parks' wildlife and natural beauty. However, the Grand Canyon still faces environmental challenges. For example, many of the area's animals are **threatened** or endangered, such as the California condor. For others, including some fish species, it is already too late. They have disappeared from the park.

The park is home to eight threatened or endangered animal species.

Tamarisk grows behind native grasses along the Little Colorado River.

Unwanted Invaders

Invasive species pose a serious threat. These are plants and animals that are not native to the park. When they spread into a new area, they upset the environment's natural balance. Tamarisk is an invasive shrub that people brought to the Grand Canyon in the early 20th century to fight erosion. The plant spreads quickly, however, and crowds out native plants. Park workers now remove many tamarisk plants in an attempt to control their spread.

Wild donkeys, called burros, were once a damaging invasive species in the park. After decades of effort to control the burro population, few remain there.

Safety on the Trail

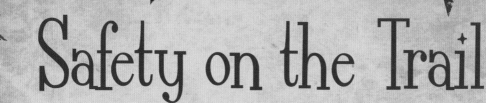

Park rangers have a challenging job in preserving the park. Much of this work involves making sure the park's hundreds of trails remain safe for visitors exploring the Grand Canyon. Weather can cause rockslides, crumbling paths, and other safety hazards. Park employees watch constantly for these dangers. Rangers close down trails, post warnings, and make repairs as necessary. This helps ensure that visitors do not get hurt as they enjoy the park. Rangers also work to educate visitors about other potential hazards, such as not drinking enough water while hiking.

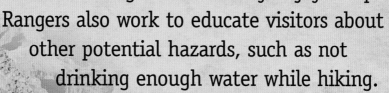

Restoring Rare Species

There are many ongoing efforts to protect the park's threatened and endangered species. For example, there were only nine wild California condors alive in 1983. Wildlife experts captured them and began raising their young in **captivity**. Beginning in the 1990s, these captive-raised condors were released into the wild near the Grand Canyon. Today, the total wild California condor population in Arizona and California has risen to more than 400. This includes almost 170 that currently live in captivity.

California condor populations have grown in recent years.

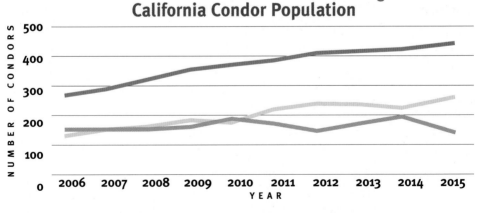

California Condor Population

NUMBER OF CONDORS

500
400
300
200
100
0

2006 2007 2008 2009 2010 2011 2012 2013 2014 2015

YEAR

KEY
▬▬ Total Condor Population   ▬▬ Wild Condor Population   ▬▬ Captive Condor Population

City lights can affect areas that are miles away.

People Problems

Increased human population around the Grand Canyon over many years has led to more cars, power plants, and other sources of air pollution. Mining operations threaten to pollute the Colorado River. Electric lights affect the park's nighttime views of the starry sky. Low-flying aircraft bring loud, unfamiliar sounds. These problems have no easy solution. But people can help the environment generally with simple steps like conserving water and electricity. With everyone's help, we can preserve the Grand Canyon and other places of natural beauty. ★

Map Mystery

At the end of a trail sits a simple-looking building designed as a place for visitors to take a break and enjoy the view. What is the building called? Follow the directions below to find the answer.

Skywalk

Colorado River

A R

Directions

1. Start at South Entrance Station.

2. Head north to Park Headquarters.

3. Travel east until you reach the Desert View Visitor Center.

4. Now hike west along the South Rim, following the Colorado River.

5. Almost there! West of Grand Canyon Village, look for a spot where you can take a rest—and solve the mystery!

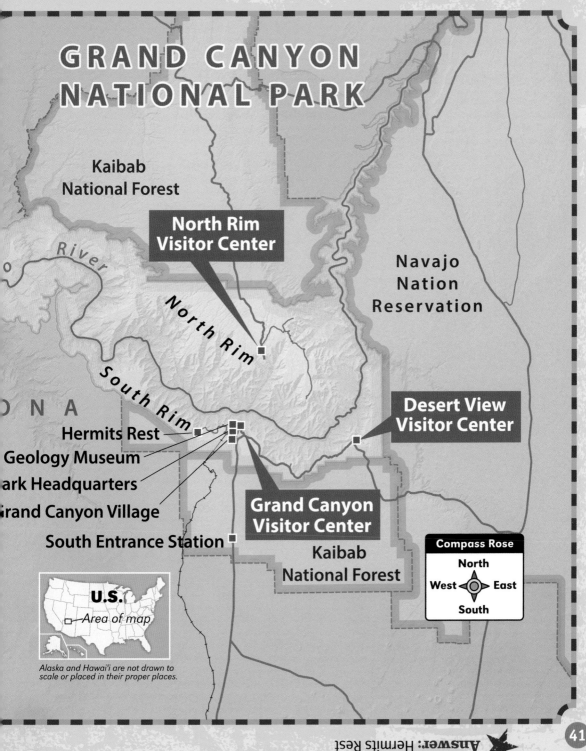

GRAND CANYON NATIONAL PARK

Kaibab
National Forest

River

North Rim

**North Rim
Visitor Center**

Navajo
Nation
Reservation

South Rim

ONA

**Desert View
Visitor Center**

Hermits Rest
Geology Museum
ark Headquarters
rand Canyon Village

**Grand Canyon
Visitor Center**

South Entrance Station

Kaibab
National Forest

U.S.
Area of map

Alaska and Hawai'i are not drawn to
scale or placed in their proper places.

Compass Rose

North

West · East

South

Be an Animal Tracker!

If you're ever in Grand Canyon National Park, keep an eye out for these animal tracks. They'll help you know which animals are in the area.

Bison
Hoof length: 5 inches (13 cm)

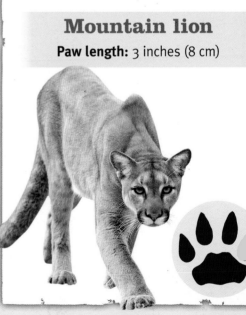

Mountain lion
Paw length: 3 inches (8 cm)

Elk

Hoof length: 3 inches (8 cm)

Mule deer

Hoof length: 3 inches (8 cm)

Bighorn sheep

Hoof length: 3 inches (8 cm)

Ringtail

Paw length: 1 inch (3 cm)

True Statistics

Length of the Grand Canyon: 277 mi. (446 km)

Total length of the Colorado River: 1,450 mi. (2,333 km)

Width of Grand Canyon at its widest point: 18 mi. (29 km)

Number of plant species in the park: More than 2,000

Number of bird species: Nearly 450

Number of mammal species: 91

Number of reptile species: About 48

Number of amphibian species: About 10

Number of known insect and arachnid species: More than 1,440

Did you find the truth?

(F) Temperatures at the bottom of the canyon are colder than those higher up.

(T) The Grand Canyon is 1 mile (1.6 kilometers) deep on average.

Resources

Books

Flynn, Sarah Wassner, and Julie Beer. *National Parks Guide U.S.A.* Washington, DC: National Geographic, 2016.

O'Connor, Jim. *Where Is the Grand Canyon?* New York: Grosset & Dunlap, 2015.

Rowell, Rebecca. *The 12 Most Amazing American Natural Wonders.* North Mankato, MN: 12-Story Library, 2015.

Visit this Scholastic website for more information on Grand Canyon National Park:

★ www.factsfornow.scholastic.com
Enter the keywords **Grand Canyon**

Important Words

archaeologists (ahr-kee-AH-luh-jists) people who study the distant past by digging up and examining its physical remains, such as old buildings, household objects, and bones

captivity (kap-TIV-i-tee) the condition of being held or trapped by people

descendants (di-SEN-duhnts) one's children, their children, and so on into the future

endangered (en-DAYN-jurd) in danger of becoming extinct, usually because of human activity

erode (i-ROHD) to wear away gradually by water or wind

expedition (ek-spuh-DISH-uhn) a long trip made for a specific purpose, such as for exploration

invertebrate (in-VUR-tuh-brit) relating to an animal without a backbone

mammal (MAM-uhl) a warm-blooded animal that has hair or fur and usually gives birth to live babies

native (NAY-tiv) living or growing naturally in a certain place

species (SPEE-sheez) one of the groups into which animals and plants are divided; members of the same species can mate and have offspring

threatened (THRET-uhnd) vulnerable, facing the possibility of becoming endangered

Index

Page numbers in **bold** indicate illustrations.

About the Author

Josh Gregory is the author of more than 100 books for kids. He has written about everything from animals to technology to history. A graduate of the University of Missouri-Columbia, he currently lives in Portland, Oregon.